THIS BOOK BELONGS TO:

Title	
Genre:		Year	
Length		Director	

ACTORS
-
-
-
-
-
-
-

AWARDS
-
-

SUMMARY

NOTES

RATINGS

Title	
Genre:	Year
Length	Director

ACTORS
-
-
-
-
-
-
-

AWARDS
-
-

SUMMARY

NOTES

Title			
Genre:		Year	
Length		Director	

ACTORS

-
-
-

-
-
-

AWARDS
-
-

SUMMARY

NOTES

RATINGS

Cast		Director	
Screen Play		Effects	
Costumes		Overall Rating	
Overall Rating			

ACTORS
-
-
-
-
-
-

AWARDS
-
-

SUMMARY

NOTES

RATINGS

Cast		Director	
Screen Play		Effects	
Costumes		Overall Rating	
Overall Rating			

ACTORS

-
-
-
-
-
-

AWARDS

-
-

SUMMARY

NOTES

RATINGS

Cast		Director	
Screen Play		Effects	
Costumes		Overall Rating	
Overall Rating			

Title	

Genre:		Year	
Length		Director	

ACTORS

-
-
-

-
-
-

AWARDS

-
-

SUMMARY

NOTES

Screen Play

Costumes

Overall Rating

Title			
Genre:		Year	
Length		Director	

ACTORS
-
-
-
-
-
-

AWARDS
-
-

SUMMARY

NOTES

RATINGS

Title	

Genre:		Year	
Length		Director	

ACTORS
-
-
-
-
-
-
-

AWARDS
-
-

SUMMARY

NOTES

Title	
Genre:		Year	
Length		Director	

ACTORS
-
-
-
-
-
-

AWARDS
-
-

SUMMARY

NOTES

RATINGS

Cast		Director	
Screen Play		Effects	
Costumes		Overall Rating	
Overall Rating			

ACTORS
-
-
-
-
-
-

AWARDS
-
-

SUMMARY

NOTES

RATINGS

Cast		Director	
Screen Play		Effects	
Costumes		Overall Rating	
Overall Rating			

ACTORS

-
-
-

-
-
-

AWARDS

-
-

SUMMARY

NOTES

RATINGS

Cast		Director	
Screen Play		Effects	
Costumes		Overall Rating	
Overall Rating			

Title	
Genre:		Year	
Length		Director	

ACTORS
-
-
-
-
-
-
-

AWARDS
-
-

SUMMARY

NOTES

RATINGS

Cast		Director	
Screen Play		Effects	
Costumes		Overall Rating	
Overall Rating			

Title	
Genre:		Year	
Length		Director	

ACTORS
-
-
-
-
-
-

AWARDS
-
-

SUMMARY

NOTES

RATINGS

Cast		Director	
Screen Play		Effects	
Costumes		Overall Rating	
Overall Rating			

Title			
Genre:		Year	
Length		Director	

ACTORS
-
-
-
-
-
-
-

AWARDS
-
-

SUMMARY

NOTES

Title			
Genre:		Year	
Length		Director	

ACTORS

-
-
-

-
-
-

AWARDS

-
-

SUMMARY

NOTES

RATINGS

Title	
Genre:		Year	
Length		Director	

ACTORS
-
-
-
-
-
-

AWARDS
-
-

SUMMARY

NOTES

RATINGS

Cast		Director	
Screen Play		Effects	
Costumes		Overall Rating	
Overall Rating			

ACTORS

-
-
-
-
-
-

AWARDS

-
-

SUMMARY

NOTES

RATINGS

Cast		Director	
Screen Play		Effects	
Costumes		Overall Rating	
Overall Rating			

Title	
Genre:		Year	
Length		Director	

ACTORS
-
-
-
-
-
-

AWARDS
-
-

SUMMARY

NOTES

RATINGS

Cast		Director	
Screen Play		Effects	
Costumes		Overall Rating	
Overall Rating			

Title			
Genre:		Year	
Length		Director	

ACTORS
-
-
-
-
-
-

AWARDS
-
-

SUMMARY

NOTES

RATINGS

Title			
Genre:		Year	
Length		Director	

ACTORS
-
-
-
-
-
-
-

AWARDS
-
-

SUMMARY

NOTES

Title				
Genre:		Year		
Length		Director		

ACTORS
-
-
-
-
-
-

AWARDS
-
-

SUMMARY

NOTES

RATINGS

Cast		Director	
Screen Play		Effects	
Costumes		Overall Rating	
Overall Rating			

Title	

Genre:		Year	
Length		Director	

ACTORS
-
-
-

-
-
-

AWARDS
-
-

SUMMARY

NOTES

RATINGS

Cast		Director	
Screen Play		Effects	
Costumes		Overall Rating	
Overall Rating			

ACTORS
-
-
-
    -
    -
    -
    -

AWARDS
-
-

SUMMARY

NOTES

RATINGS

Cast		Director	
Screen Play		Effects	
Costumes		Overall Rating	
Overall Rating			

Title	
Genre:		Year	
Length		Director	

ACTORS
-
-
-
-
-
-
-

AWARDS
-
-

SUMMARY

NOTES

RATINGS

Cast		Director	
Screen Play		Effects	
Costumes		Overall Rating	
Overall Rating			

Title	
Genre:		Year	
Length		Director	

ACTORS
-
-
-
-
-
-

AWARDS
-
-

SUMMARY

NOTES

RATINGS

Cast		Director	
Screen Play		Effects	
Costumes		Overall Rating	
Overall Rating			

Title	

Genre:		Year	
Length		Director	

ACTORS
-
-
-
-
-
-

AWARDS
-
-

SUMMARY

NOTES

RATINGS

Cast		Director	
Screen Play		Effects	
Costumes		Overall Rating	
Overall Rating			

Title	
Genre:		Year	
Length		Director	

ACTORS
-
-
-
-
-
-
-

AWARDS
-
-

SUMMARY

NOTES

RATINGS

Cast		Director	
Screen Play		Effects	
Costumes		Overall Rating	
Overall Rating			

ACTORS
-
-
-
-
-
-

AWARDS
-
-

SUMMARY

NOTES

RATINGS

Cast		Director	
Screen Play		Effects	
Costumes		Overall Rating	
Overall Rating			

ACTORS

-
-
-

-
-
-

-
-

SUMMARY

NOTES

RATINGS

Cast		Director	
Screen Play		Effects	
Costumes		Overall Rating	
Overall Rating			

Title	
Genre:		Year	
Length		Director	

ACTORS
-
-
-
-
-
-
-

AWARDS
-
-

SUMMARY

NOTES

RATINGS

Cast		Director	
Screen Play		Effects	
Costumes		Overall Rating	
Overall Rating			

Title	

Genre:		Year	
Length		Director	

ACTORS
-
-
-
-
-
-

AWARDS
-
-

SUMMARY

NOTES

RATINGS

Cast		Director	
Screen Play		Effects	
Costumes		Overall Rating	
Overall Rating			

Title	
Genre:	Year
Length	Director

ACTORS
-
-
-
-
-
-
-

AWARDS
-
-

SUMMARY

NOTES

Title	
Genre:		Year	
Length		Director	

ACTORS
-
-
-
-
-
-
-

AWARDS
-
-

SUMMARY

NOTES

RATINGS

Cast		Director	
Screen Play		Effects	
Costumes		Overall Rating	
Overall Rating			

ACTORS
-
-
-
-
-
-

AWARDS
-
-

SUMMARY

NOTES

RATINGS

Cast		Director	
Screen Play		Effects	
Costumes		Overall Rating	
Overall Rating			

ACTORS
-
-
-

-
-
-
-

AWARDS	• •

SUMMARY

NOTES

RATINGS

Cast		Director	
Screen Play		Effects	
Costumes		Overall Rating	
Overall Rating			

Title	

Genre:		Year	
Length		Director	

ACTORS
-
-
-
-
-
-
-

AWARDS
-
-

SUMMARY

NOTES

RATINGS

Cast		Director	
Screen Play		Effects	
Costumes		Overall Rating	
Overall Rating			

Title	

Genre:		Year	
Length		Director	

ACTORS
-
-
-
-
-
-
-

AWARDS
-
-

SUMMARY

NOTES

RATINGS

Cast		Director	
Screen Play		Effects	
Costumes		Overall Rating	
Overall Rating			

Title	

Genre:		Year	
Length		Director	

ACTORS
-
-
-
-
-
-

AWARDS
-
-

SUMMARY

NOTES

RATINGS

Cast		Director	
Screen Play		Effects	
Costumes		Overall Rating	
Overall Rating			

Title	
Genre:	Year
Length	Director

ACTORS
-
-
-
-
-
-
-

AWARDS
-
-

SUMMARY

NOTES

RATINGS

Cast		Director	
Screen Play		Effects	
Costumes		Overall Rating	
Overall Rating			

ACTORS
-
-
-
-
-
-

AWARDS
-
-

SUMMARY

NOTES

RATINGS

Cast		Director	
Screen Play		Effects	
Costumes		Overall Rating	
Overall Rating			

ACTORS

-
-
-
-
-
-

AWARDS

-
-

SUMMARY

NOTES

RATINGS

Cast		Director	
Screen Play		Effects	
Costumes		Overall Rating	
Overall Rating			

Title	

Genre:		Year	
Length		Director	

ACTORS

-
-
-

-
-
-

AWARDS

-
-

SUMMARY

NOTES

RATINGS

Cast		Director	
Screen Play		Effects	
Costumes		Overall Rating	
Overall Rating			

Title	
Genre:		Year	
Length		Director	

ACTORS
-
-
-
-
-
-

AWARDS
-
-

SUMMARY

NOTES

RATINGS

Cast		Director	
Screen Play		Effects	
Costumes		Overall Rating	
Overall Rating			

Title	
Genre:		Year	
Length		Director	

ACTORS
-
-
-
-
-
-

AWARDS
-
-

SUMMARY

NOTES

RATINGS

Cast		Director	
Screen Play		Effects	
Costumes		Overall Rating	
Overall Rating			

Title			
Genre:		Year	
Length		Director	

ACTORS
-
-
-

-
-
-

AWARDS
-
-

SUMMARY

NOTES

RATINGS

Cast		Director	
Screen Play		Effects	
Costumes		Overall Rating	
Overall Rating			

ACTORS
-
-
-
-
-
-

AWARDS
-
-

SUMMARY

NOTES

RATINGS

Cast		Director	
Screen Play		Effects	
Costumes		Overall Rating	
Overall Rating			

ACTORS

-
-
-
-
-
-

AWARDS

-
-

SUMMARY

NOTES

RATINGS

Cast		Director	
Screen Play		Effects	
Costumes		Overall Rating	
Overall Rating			

Title	
Genre:		Year	
Length		Director	

ACTORS
-
-
-
-
-
-
-

AWARDS
-
-

SUMMARY

NOTES

RATINGS

Cast		Director	
Screen Play		Effects	
Costumes		Overall Rating	
Overall Rating			

Title			
Genre:		Year	
Length		Director	

ACTORS

-
-
-

-
-
-
-

AWARDS

-
-

SUMMARY

NOTES

RATINGS

Cast		Director	
Screen Play		Effects	
Costumes		Overall Rating	
Overall Rating			

Title	

Genre:		Year	
Length		Director	

ACTORS
-
-
-
-
-
-
-

AWARDS
-
-

SUMMARY

NOTES

Screen Play	
Costumes	
Overall Rating	

Title	
Genre:		Year	
Length		Director	

ACTORS
-
-
-
-
-
-
-

AWARDS
-
-

SUMMARY

NOTES

RATINGS

Cast		Director	
Screen Play		Effects	
Costumes		Overall Rating	
Overall Rating			

ACTORS

-
-
-

-
-
-

AWARDS

-
-

SUMMARY

NOTES

RATINGS

Cast		Director	
Screen Play		Effects	
Costumes		Overall Rating	
Overall Rating			

ACTORS

-
-
-
-
-
-

AWARDS

-
-

SUMMARY

NOTES

RATINGS

Cast		Director	
Screen Play		Effects	
Costumes		Overall Rating	
Overall Rating			

Title	
Genre:		Year	
Length		Director	

ACTORS
-
-
-
-
-
-
-

AWARDS
-
-

SUMMARY

NOTES

RATINGS

Cast		Director	
Screen Play		Effects	
Costumes		Overall Rating	
Overall Rating			

Title	
Genre:		Year	
Length		Director	

ACTORS
-
-
-
-
-
-
-

AWARDS
-
-

SUMMARY

NOTES

RATINGS

Cast		Director	
Screen Play		Effects	
Costumes		Overall Rating	
Overall Rating			

Title	
Genre:	Year
Length	Director

ACTORS
-
-
-
-
-
-

AWARDS
-
-

SUMMARY

NOTES

Overall Rating

Title	
Genre:		Year	
Length		Director	

ACTORS
-
-
-
-
-
-
-

AWARDS
-
-

SUMMARY

NOTES

RATINGS

Cast		Director	
Screen Play		Effects	
Costumes		Overall Rating	
Overall Rating			

ACTORS
-
-
-

-
-
-
-

AWARDS
-
-

SUMMARY

NOTES

RATINGS

Cast		Director	
Screen Play		Effects	
Costumes		Overall Rating	
Overall Rating			

ACTORS

-
-
-
-
-
-

AWARDS

-
-

SUMMARY

NOTES

RATINGS

Cast		Director	
Screen Play		Effects	
Costumes		Overall Rating	
Overall Rating			

Title			
Genre:		Year	
Length		Director	

ACTORS
-
-
-
-
-
-
-

AWARDS
-
-

SUMMARY

NOTES

RATINGS

Cast		Director	
Screen Play		Effects	
Costumes		Overall Rating	
Overall Rating			

Title	

Genre:		Year	
Length		Director	

ACTORS
-
-
-

-
-
-

AWARDS
-
-

SUMMARY

NOTES

RATINGS

Cast		Director	
Screen Play		Effects	
Costumes		Overall Rating	
Overall Rating			

Title	
Genre:		Year	
Length		Director	

ACTORS
-
-
-
-
-
-
-

AWARDS
-
-

SUMMARY

NOTES

RATINGS

Cast		Director	
Screen Play		Effects	
Costumes		Overall Rating	
Overall Rating			

Title	

Genre:		Year	
Length		Director	

ACTORS
-
-
-
-
-
-

AWARDS
-
-

SUMMARY

NOTES

RATINGS

Cast		Director	
Screen Play		Effects	
Costumes		Overall Rating	
Overall Rating			

ACTORS
-
-
-
-
-
-

AWARDS
-
-

SUMMARY

NOTES

RATINGS

Cast		Director	
Screen Play		Effects	
Costumes		Overall Rating	
Overall Rating			

			Year	
Length			Director	

ACTORS

-
-
-

-
-
-
-

	• •	

SUMMARY

NOTES

RATINGS

Cast		Director		
Screen Play		Effects		
Costumes		Overall Rating		
Overall Rating				

Title			
Genre:		Year	
Length		Director	

ACTORS
-
-
-
-
-
-

AWARDS
-
-

SUMMARY

NOTES

RATINGS

Cast		Director	
Screen Play		Effects	
Costumes		Overall Rating	
Overall Rating			

Title	

Genre:		Year	
Length		Director	

ACTORS
-
-
-

-
-
-
-

AWARDS
-
-

SUMMARY

NOTES

RATINGS

Cast		Director	
Screen Play		Effects	
Costumes		Overall Rating	
Overall Rating			

Title			
Genre:		Year	
Length		Director	

ACTORS
-
-
-
-
-
-

AWARDS
-
-

SUMMARY

NOTES

Screen Play

Costumes

Overall Rating

Title	

Genre:		Year	
Length		Director	

ACTORS
-
-
-
-
-
-
-

AWARDS
-
-

SUMMARY

NOTES

RATINGS

Cast		Director	
Screen Play		Effects	
Costumes		Overall Rating	
Overall Rating			

ACTORS

-
-
-
-
-
-

AWARDS

-
-

SUMMARY

NOTES

RATINGS

Cast		Director	
Screen Play		Effects	
Costumes		Overall Rating	
Overall Rating			

Title	

Genre:		Year	
Length		Director	

ACTORS
-
-
-
-
-
-

AWARDS
-
-

SUMMARY

NOTES

RATINGS

Cast		Director	
Screen Play		Effects	
Costumes		Overall Rating	
Overall Rating			

Title	

Genre:		Year	
Length		Director	

ACTORS

-
-
-

-
-
-

AWARDS

-
-

SUMMARY

NOTES

RATINGS

Cast		Director	
Screen Play		Effects	
Costumes		Overall Rating	
Overall Rating			

Title	
Genre:		Year	
Length		Director	

ACTORS

-
-
-
-
-
-
-

AWARDS

-
-

SUMMARY

NOTES

RATINGS

Cast		Director	
Screen Play		Effects	
Costumes		Overall Rating	
Overall Rating			

Title			
Genre:		Year	
Length		Director	

ACTORS
-
-
-
-
-
-

AWARDS
-
-

SUMMARY

NOTES

RATINGS

Overall Rating	

Title	

Genre:		Year	
Length		Director	

ACTORS
-
-
-
-
-
-
-

AWARDS
-
-

SUMMARY

NOTES

RATINGS

Cast		Director	
Screen Play		Effects	
Costumes		Overall Rating	
Overall Rating			

Title

ACTORS
-
-
-
-
-
-

AWARDS
-
-

SUMMARY

NOTES

RATINGS

Cast		Director	
Screen Play		Effects	
Costumes		Overall Rating	
Overall Rating			

ACTORS

-
-
-
-
-
-

AWARDS

-
-

SUMMARY

NOTES

RATINGS

Cast		Director	
Screen Play		Effects	
Costumes		Overall Rating	
Overall Rating			

Title	
Genre:		Year	
Length		Director	

ACTORS
-
-
-
-
-
-
-

AWARDS
-
-

SUMMARY

NOTES

RATINGS

Cast		Director	
Screen Play		Effects	
Costumes		Overall Rating	
Overall Rating			

Title	
Genre:		Year	
Length		Director	

ACTORS
-
-
-
-
-
-
-

AWARDS
-
-

SUMMARY

NOTES

RATINGS

Cast		Director	
Screen Play		Effects	
Costumes		Overall Rating	
Overall Rating			

Title			
Genre:		Year	
Length		Director	

ACTORS

-
-
-

-
-
-
-

AWARDS

-
-

SUMMARY

NOTES

Title	

Genre:		Year	
Length		Director	

ACTORS
-
-
-

-
-
-

AWARDS
-
-

SUMMARY

NOTES

RATINGS

Cast		Director	
Screen Play		Effects	
Costumes		Overall Rating	
Overall Rating			

ACTORS

-
-
-
-
-
-

AWARDS

-
-

SUMMARY

NOTES

RATINGS

Cast		Director	
Screen Play		Effects	
Costumes		Overall Rating	
Overall Rating			

ACTORS

-
-
-

-
-
-
-

AWARDS

-
-

SUMMARY

NOTES

RATINGS

Cast		Director	
Screen Play		Effects	
Costumes		Overall Rating	
Overall Rating			

Title	

Genre:		Year	
Length		Director	

ACTORS
-
-
-
-
-
-

AWARDS
-
-

SUMMARY

NOTES

RATINGS

Cast		Director	
Screen Play		Effects	
Costumes		Overall Rating	
Overall Rating			

Title	
Genre:		Year	
Length		Director	

ACTORS
-
-
-
-
-
-
-

AWARDS
-
-

SUMMARY

NOTES

RATINGS

Title			
Genre:		Year	
Length		Director	

ACTORS
-
-
-
-
-
-
-

AWARDS
-
-

SUMMARY

NOTES

Title			
Genre:		Year	
Length		Director	

ACTORS
-
-
-
-
-
-
-

AWARDS
-
-

SUMMARY

NOTES

RATINGS

Director

ACTORS

-
-
-
-
-
-
-

AWARDS

-
-

SUMMARY

NOTES

RATINGS

Cast		Director	
Screen Play		Effects	
Costumes		Overall Rating	
Overall Rating			

ACTORS

-
-
-
-
-
-

AWARDS

-
-

SUMMARY

NOTES

RATINGS

Cast		Director	
Screen Play		Effects	
Costumes		Overall Rating	
Overall Rating			

Title	
Genre:		Year	
Length		Director	

ACTORS
-
-
-
-
-
-
-

AWARDS
-
-

SUMMARY

NOTES

RATINGS

Cast		Director	
Screen Play		Effects	
Costumes		Overall Rating	
Overall Rating			

Title	
Genre:		Year	
Length		Director	

ACTORS
-
-
-
-
-
-
-

AWARDS
-
-

SUMMARY

NOTES

RATINGS

Cast		Director	
Screen Play		Effects	
Costumes		Overall Rating	
Overall Rating			

Title	

Genre:		Year	
Length		Director	

ACTORS
-
-
-
-
-
-
-

AWARDS
-
-

SUMMARY

NOTES

RATINGS

Cast		Director	
Screen Play		Effects	
Costumes		Overall Rating	
Overall Rating			

Title			
Genre:		Year	
Length		Director	

ACTORS
-
-
-

-
-
-

AWARDS
-
-

NOTES

RATINGS

Cast		Director	
Screen Play		Effects	
Costumes		Overall Rating	
Overall Rating			

Title	

Genre:		Year	
Length		Director	

ACTORS
-
-
-
-
-
-

AWARDS
-
-

SUMMARY

NOTES

RATINGS

Cast		Director	
Screen Play		Effects	
Costumes		Overall Rating	
Overall Rating			

ACTORS

-
-
-

-
-
-

AWARDS

-
-

SUMMARY

NOTES

RATINGS

Cast		Director	
Screen Play		Effects	
Costumes		Overall Rating	
Overall Rating			

Title			
Genre:		Year	
Length		Director	

ACTORS

-
-
-

-
-
-

AWARDS

-
-

SUMMARY

NOTES

Screen Play

Costumes

Overall Rating

Title	
Genre:		Year	
Length		Director	

ACTORS
-
-
-
-
-
-

AWARDS
-
-

SUMMARY

NOTES

RATINGS

Title			
Genre:		Year	
Length		Director	

ACTORS
-
-
-
-
-
-
-

AWARDS
-
-

SUMMARY

NOTES

Overall Rating

Title	

Genre:		Year	
Length		Director	

ACTORS
-
-
-
-
-
-
-

AWARDS
-
-

SUMMARY

NOTES

RATINGS

Cast		Director	
Screen Play		Effects	
Costumes		Overall Rating	
Overall Rating			

Title	
Genre:		Year	
Length		Director	

ACTORS

-
-
-
-
-
-
-

AWARDS

-
-

SUMMARY

NOTES

RATINGS

Cast		Director	
Screen Play		Effects	
Costumes		Overall Rating	
Overall Rating			

ACTORS

-
-
-
-
-
-

AWARDS

-
-

SUMMARY

NOTES

RATINGS

Cast		Director	
Screen Play		Effects	
Costumes		Overall Rating	
Overall Rating			

Title	

Genre:		Year	
Length		Director	

ACTORS
-
-
-

-
-
-

AWARDS
-
-

SUMMARY

NOTES

RATINGS

Cast		Director	
Screen Play		Effects	
Costumes		Overall Rating	
Overall Rating			

Title	

Genre:		Year	
Length		Director	

ACTORS
-
-
-
-
-
-

AWARDS
-
-

SUMMARY

NOTES

RATINGS

Cast		Director	
Screen Play		Effects	
Costumes		Overall Rating	
Overall Rating			

Title	
Genre:		Year	
Length		Director	

ACTORS
-
-
-
-
-
-
-

AWARDS
-
-

SUMMARY

NOTES

RATINGS

Overall Rating

Title			
Genre:		Year	
Length		Director	

ACTORS
-
-
-
-
-
-
-

AWARDS
-
-

SUMMARY

NOTES

RATINGS

Cast		Director	
Screen Play		Effects	
Costumes		Overall Rating	
Overall Rating			

ACTORS
-
-
-
-
-
-
-

AWARDS
-
-

SUMMARY

NOTES

RATINGS

Cast		Director	
Screen Play		Effects	
Costumes		Overall Rating	
Overall Rating			

Title	
Genre:		Year	
Length		Director	

ACTORS
-
-
-
-
-
-
-

AWARDS
-
-

SUMMARY

NOTES

RATINGS

Cast		Director	
Screen Play		Effects	
Costumes		Overall Rating	
Overall Rating			

Title				
Genre:		Year		
Length		Director		

ACTORS

-
-
-

-
-
-
-

AWARDS

-
-

SUMMARY

NOTES

Overall Rating

Title	
Genre:		Year	
Length		Director	

ACTORS
-
-
-
-
-
-
-

AWARDS
-
-

SUMMARY

NOTES

RATINGS

Title			
Genre:		Year	
Length		Director	

ACTORS

-
-
-

-
-
-
-

AWARDS

-
-

SUMMARY

NOTES

RATINGS

Title	
Genre:	Year
Length	Director

ACTORS
-
-
-
-
-
-
-

AWARDS
-
-
-

SUMMARY

NOTES

RATINGS

ACTORS
-
-
-
-
-
-
-
-

SUMMARY

NOTES

RATINGS

Cast		Director	
Screen Play		Effects	
Costumes		Overall Rating	
Overall Rating			

ACTORS
-
-
-
-
-
-

AWARDS
-
-

SUMMARY

NOTES

RATINGS

Cast		Director	
Screen Play		Effects	
Costumes		Overall Rating	
Overall Rating			

Title	

Genre:		Year	
Length		Director	

ACTORS
-
-
-

-
-
-
-

AWARDS
-
-
-

SUMMARY

NOTES

RATINGS

Cast		Director	
Screen Play		Effects	
Costumes		Overall Rating	
Overall Rating			

Title	
Genre:		Year	
Length		Director	

ACTORS
-
-
-
-
-
-
-

AWARDS
-
-

SUMMARY

NOTES

RATINGS

Title			
Genre:		Year	
Length		Director	

ACTORS

-
-
-

-
-
-
-

AWARDS

-
-

SUMMARY

NOTES

Overall Rating

Title	
Genre:		Year	
Length		Director	

ACTORS
-
-
-
-
-
-
-

AWARDS
-
-

SUMMARY

NOTES

RATINGS

Cast		Director	
Screen Play		Effects	
Costumes		Overall Rating	
Overall Rating			

ACTORS
-
-
-
-
-
-

AWARDS
-
-

SUMMARY

NOTES

RATINGS

Cast		Director	
Screen Play		Effects	
Costumes		Overall Rating	
Overall Rating			

ACTORS

-
-
-
-
-
-

AWARDS

-
-

SUMMARY

NOTES

RATINGS

Cast		Director	
Screen Play		Effects	
Costumes		Overall Rating	
Overall Rating			